The MBA Survival Guide: *How* *prosper at a top 25 MBA pro*

Intro/My background

Before you dive in, I'm sure you all want to know a little bit about who is giving you advice, right? I graduated from my MBA program a couple of years ago and am currently working in Finance for a Fortune 500 company in the Midwest. One of the "extracurricular" responsibilities that I'm involved with for my company is heading up the MBA campus recruiting for the school that I graduated from. I'm the guy they send to campus to rev up the troops and get them foaming at the mouth for an interview, let alone a job. I get the joy of free, expensive recruiting dinners and the miserableness of doing 14 interviews back to back, and that's only after I review a stack of résumés and cover letters as tall as me (and I'm 6'2"). More importantly for you, I know what companies look for in their MBA talent and how senior executives approach interviews, and can hopefully give some useful advice based on my experience. I'll keep my school and character names anonymous to protect the innocent, but I can tell you that it was a top 25 program; most of my experiences and advice will be relevant to other top programs as well.

Prior to coming back to school I had a checkered work experience that involved the highs of owning my own business in college and raking in more money than I knew what to do with at the time (or than I do now for that matter), down to the lows of being laid off during the great recession as companies just weren't shelling out the cash for IT consultants and new software implementations. (Can't say I blame them.) The gist of it is that I have owned my own products business on the wholesale and retail side, managed a region of a private education business owned by someone else, and also worked in private banking and IT consulting prior to getting my MBA.

Admissions Process

Application Story Consistency:

The admissions process is pretty much what you would expect and are familiar with from undergrad, except that there is an interview involved. However, you need to put a little more thought into the content of your application this time around. Business schools care about one thing, and it is their rankings. Now, just how do they maintain or improve their rankings? A few of the main factors that make up that magical number that every business school dean is striving to improve include:

- Student satisfaction surveys
- Admissions statistics: entering class undergraduate GPAs, GMAT scores, diversity in ethnic and geographic profile, etc.
- Job placement: percentage of students with offers at varying points up to and past graduation and the quality (salary) of those jobs

At this point you might be thinking, "OK, my stats are what they are in regards to undergrad GPA and GMAT score, what the hell can I do for the rest of those items?" Job placement is key. Try to stay with me on this as it seems a little counterintuitive, and most people think of this as something that you should be worried about towards the end of your MBA. What you need to do here is convince the school that you know what you want to do after graduation, have a plan to get there, and that it is all reasonable. At this stage in the game they're thinking about whether you are going to hurt or help them in the job placement stats. You need to convince them that you're going to kick some serious tail here, as opposed to being the weird alum that graduated last year without a job and that now spends most of his time hanging out in the library and showing up to events for current students. We had one of those guys and referred to him as Quasimodo because, well, he kind of looked like the hunchback and he'd clearly overstayed his welcome. You need to convince admissions that you won't become that guy (or girl) and become the running joke of your successor classes. Also, if you do well on your job search and get the type of job you are looking for while making more money than you can dream of, guess what -- you'll probably be happy and be very nice when filling out those student satisfaction surveys, won't you?

So exactly how do you convince the admission team that you know what you want to do and will do well in the job search? You need to craft all of your essays, no matter what they are about, to have the same or a similar theme. This could be, for example, your passion for helping clients and working in healthcare, which is why you want to work in life sciences consulting, administration for a large provider, for a pharmaceutical company, etc. You also need to convince admissions that their school and MBA program is the right one to get you where you want to go. Mention a specific teacher or class that you really want to take. Name specific companies that you want to work for and mention that you were very pleased to see some of the most recent years' job placement reports showing that students from their program actually went to work at those companies. Not only does this show that you have a goal and have done your research, but that the program can likely get you where you want to go.

If you want to work in private equity and that is your lifelong dream, fantastic. However, if the school that you are applying to had 0 out of 300 students go into private equity from the last graduating class and no PE firms come recruit at the school, well, you'll have your work cut out for you. If you want to stick to that route and are a career switcher without the background for private equity, you may want to consider pivoting your application theme to say that you know most PE firms hire those with large investment bank experience, and that is why you want to work for JPMorgan or Goldman Sachs after graduation for some time before making the switch to private equity. If the school doesn't have a mentionable amount of banks that come recruit on campus or students that go work in the field after graduation, well then, either consider a different MBA program that better suits your needs, or at least alter your application theme to one that is a better fit for the program that you are applying to. Admissions definitely notices when you have done your research on their program as opposed to just "mailing it in", so to speak, when it comes to the application process.

Program research weaved into your application theme doesn't stop in relation to jobs. You also need to do some research on the program and what student life is like. Business schools are themselves a business, and like most other large companies that you will likely be seeking employment with, you need to consider this process the same. Business schools and large companies alike have their own unique culture. You can learn about it by reading the canned lines they have on their websites, all of which are likely to include words like "Collaborative" and "Diverse", and you can also speak to current students or recent graduates. If you go this route, make sure you find an appropriate way to bring up the additional research, and of course, go into detail about why their culture appeals to you and how you are a perfect fit for it.

Interviews:

What I can tell you here is pretty standard interview advice and will serve you well no matter what you are interviewing for. To start off, the interview can either be done over the phone or in person. The schools will tell you that it doesn't matter which way you choose, but I honestly find that hard to believe. If you can make the interview in person, do it. This will show your commitment and seriousness about their program. It is also a great way for you to learn more about the program, as most schools will set you up for a sort of campus visit as opposed to just an interview. You will of course have your interview, but then will also have the chance to sit in on a class, as well as have lunch with some current students. While it will be a brief glimpse into student life, it's a good way to get a feel for the student culture and program overall. Also keep in mind that while the class visit and lunch is not an interview, it *is* a chance for you to screw up. The students that you meet with will likely need to fill out and submit a brief form on their visit with you, and all will recommend you unless you give them a clear reason not to. Overall, just be yourself, and have some authentic and genuine questions ready, but try not to ask anyone about where to go out and find the hot undergrads as you play with the wedding ring on your finger.

For your interview, be ready to answer some of these basic questions.

- Why do you want to come back to school for your MBA?
- Why is now a good time to get your MBA?
- Why is [insert the school you're interviewing with] a good choice for your MBA?
- What do you want to do after school and why?

You will obviously need to answer other questions as well, but be prepared for those basic questions that you likely answered fifty times in your application materials. Are you starting to notice a theme here? Consistency is key! Make sure that the answers you give to the questions this time around are consistent with what you said in your application. Brush up on all those essays that you sent in, and keep all of your answers along a similar theme. Most interviews will be just thirty to forty-five minutes long, with them leaving about ten minutes for you to ask them questions, so don't sweat this too much. They won't have time to ask you too many questions, and the ones that they do will be very easy and conversational. They're not trying to trip you up or stump you here, but to get to know you better. Also, as mentioned before, they are trying to see if you are a good fit for the culture of the program and to see if you will do well in the job search; interview skills are key for this.

The last piece of the interview is when *you* get to ask them questions. Make sure you have a few good questions prepared ahead of time and don't forget them. Also, don't ask them a question that you can easily find the answer to, or something as canned and generic as the few bulleted questions I listed above. Ask well-thought-out questions that they aren't likely to hear from everyone else. Don't sweat the interview too much. If they are interviewing you, then they are obviously interested in you as a candidate and you have a good shot at getting in. These will be some of the easiest interviews of your life, since it's all about you! Just relax and be yourself. In my interview I botched the last name of my student guide who I sat in on a class with, and it was in fact the last name of my interviewer. She seemed a little confused and I didn't even realize the mistake until afterwards. In my mind, I'm thinking that I'm done for, clearly showing I didn't prepare to the point that I don't even know my interviewer's last name! However, the rest of the interview went well and I got news of my acceptance within a week, so the moral of the story is that it's the home stretch of the process -- relax and you'll be fine.

Acceptance and Offer Negotiation:

Congratulations, you've been accepted! So now what do you do? Well, that depends on a few things. Your offer will either be a straight acceptance or it will come with some type of scholarship or aid attached. Whether it comes with any scholarship money or not, you can always try to get some. I am not timid at all when it comes to negotiating, asking for raises, or anything of the like. However, when it came to being accepted into the program of my choice I just didn't want to mess it up and was happy with my offer. Bad choice! After learning later on about what my friends with crappier GPAs, GMATs, job experience, and any combination of the three got in aid compared to me, I quickly learned my lesson. Even my career services advisors told me that I should've been able to push for something.

What you need to do here is approach this just like a job negotiation. Hopefully you have some leverage that you will be able to use to your advantage. Did you get into a higher-ranked program or a better school? Did any other school offer you scholarship money and the one you want to go to didn't, or other schools simply offered you more? Use this to your advantage. You are already accepted, so you know that they want you. As in any job offer negotiation, you need to approach this in a tactful way and be very appreciative and express your excitement at the opportunity. However, it is all right to mention your other alternatives and that you would like them to match or beat them if that is your desire -- you may be surprised and get what you're asking for.

Orientation

Program Sponsored Events:

So you're ready to go back to school and start your MBA? Well, first you'll need to get through the several days to week-long orientation process before you can dive in and hit the books! Orientation can be fun or a nightmare, depending on what type of person you are. It is basically several days of forced networking and teamwork. So if you love to talk about yourself and meet new people, this is your time to shine. However, this means that if you generally *dislike* meeting new people and having to pretend to care about their oh-so-interesting past work experience and future aspirations, then this won't exactly be enjoyable for you. For the most part you will need to attend every event. While some may technically be optional, even if you hate this type of thing, I highly recommend going to all that you can to meet as many people in the program as possible. You will be forced to work with them ad nauseam in team settings throughout your time in school anyways, so you might as well get to know them now. Besides, as is the case in most social settings, people tend to make friendships that form and solidify at the start of a new experience.

The events will range broadly, from purely social to somewhat academic and team-oriented in nature. One of our events was organized by a group of change management consultants that worked for a company started by, and who were all themselves, former Navy or Air Force pilots. As you can imagine, the task at hand was around some type of military attack and defense strategy based on certain sets of rules and limited resources. My advice here is don't try too hard and shoehorn yourself into the "leader" position as most people often do. I've seen too many times where some alpha male or outspoken woman tries to run the show because that's what they think being a leader means, and it just turns the whole thing into a disaster. Step up if you are clearly needed, otherwise just relax; remember, it's just a meaningless orientation game.

During this particular event, one of the guys in my group actually used to work for the CIA as a contractor, helping them develop very similar strategies. Instead of actually helping out he played the "too cool for school" card and spent most of the time talking about how unrealistic and ridiculous the scenario was, this would never happen, these resources would be different, blah blah blah. I'll give you a general rule of thumb for these events, or really life in general: try not to be a dick.

Even in the academic or teamwork-related events, there is still always some type of networking or getting-to-know-people piece to the event. Remember the setting you are in and that not everybody here is going to be your best bud. Before the day kicked off, we were all told to share an interesting or unique fact about ourselves with the table that we were placed at. Typically in these situations the responses tend to relate to some type of sport, an entrepreneurial achievement, or a weird hobby. However, we had one dumbass at our table that thought it was a great idea to brag about how he had been arrested three times in his life so far. Cool story, bro! As soon as the facilitator asked the room of several hundred people to have each table share with the whole room the most interesting thing heard at their table, this guy started to freak out. His face turned red as hell as he begged the whole table to keep his story to themselves, that he didn't disclose it on his admissions application and that it didn't come up in the background check, etc. etc. Nobody cared about his past, but it was pretty funny to watch him squirm. You could see the instant backfire of the kid with the privileged upbringing thinking he's cool for having a criminal past. Anyways, I digress. The moral of the story? Always know your audience.

While I haven't exactly painted the most exciting picture of orientation (you can probably tell that I'm one of the guys that does *not* like forced conversations and networking), it isn't all bad. Our school had an MBA golf tournament event that was a lot of fun. What if you don't play golf? No worries, this wasn't exactly my finest day on the links, nor anyone else's for that matter. I think "MBA golf tournament" was just a code word for "complete shitshow". Our event started off with a nice lunch at the clubhouse, with a couple of casual tasty and frosty adult beverages for the hot summer day. The second-year student facilitators started to mention stories from last year's event, as well as outline very specific things that we were not allowed to do, like end up in the clubhouse pond. Apparently, after the prior year's shenanigans we were not invited back to whatever course their tournament took place at.

I was a little confused at that point. I mean, I know I can generally hold my own better than others when it comes to drinking, thanks to my undergrad education at one of America's finest public universities, but I just didn't see that happening after a few beers at lunch. However, as soon as lunch was over it became perfectly clear what type of day we were about to have. After walking out of the clubhouse, we saw that they had all of our carts lined up; we were able to pick our partners in advance but were teamed up randomly with another pair for our foursomes. Each cart contained signs with our names and our pairs, sitting next to a glistening case of beer. What a beautiful sight! Those that didn't play golf but that wanted to be involved in the event were tasked with driving the beer cart in case people needed refills. However, instead of politely seeing if people needed more beer, they took a Gestapo-style approach to their job and drove around the course practically forcing shot-gunned beers and chugged Smirnoff Ices on site! As you can imagine, the day turned into a scene from the movie *Beerfest* and I think the winners of the "tournament" won more due to the fact that they actually played a full eighteen holes as opposed to having anything that resembled a decent score. Just another example of why you should attend all of the events if possible. This one was optional and didn't seem all that exciting to me based on my terrible golf game and initial impression that it was going to be a real golf tournament, but it ended up being a damn good time and a much more fun and natural way to meet and get to know people.

Social Events:

Some of the events mentioned in the previous section were more social in nature than academic, but here we can talk about the purely social events that are not sponsored or organized by the program. My MBA program, and I believe most others, try to offer ways for the classes to connect prior to actually beginning their MBA. Ours was done through an MBA class-wide Facebook group that was set up, I think by the school, however I honestly can't remember and it may have been set up by a student using the full-class email list that we were all provided. In either case, it's definitely another one of those things that you should look to be involved in if you want to get the most out of your MBA in terms of both connecting with your classmates and being able to go out and blow off some steam every once in a while. You'll likely hear about a few happy hours and some pretty good parties through whatever type of media connection your class uses (Facebook, mass email list, etc.). Try not to be the crazy guy that is posting forty different things for every two that other random people in the group post. If there are 100 posts in the group around fun things to do or general conversation, don't be the guy who makes 60% of those posts! Everyone will already hate you and think that you're annoying as hell before they even meet you.

If your class seems to be off to a lame start, instead of waiting for someone to find something to do, set it up yourself! I met some of my best friends throughout the two years of completing my MBA at a party that was kicked off before classes even started. You'll meet all types of people in your program, and therefore you'll come across all types of social events. Nearly everyone will go to the first few just to meet people since they're likely bored to tears, having moved to a new city without really knowing anyone, but then attendance will start to taper off a bit based on what friends they've made and what they like to do. If you're the type of person who wants to relive college and go to keg parties, then you probably won't want to go to a classmate's party where the excitement of the night is wine and cheese, and vice versa. However, at least at the beginning you never know what you're going to get in terms of some of these events, so go to as many as you can. You may be pleasantly surprised, as I was with the golf tournament.

Internship Recruiting

It might seem odd to a lot of you that I am going to start talking about internship recruiting before I go into student life and academics. There's a reason for this: namely, recruiting starts early and if you have a specific job in mind, you need to get after it and have a head start, even before your classes begin!

Networking and Informational Interviews:

I mentioned above that you should start recruiting before classes even start. Get started on the networking piece and try to get to know people at the companies that you might be interested in. For example, if you know that you want to work in strategy consulting, specifically for McKinsey, Bain, or the Boston Consulting Group (as does the rest of your MBA class, most likely), then try to reach out to speak to people in a practice group (industrials, healthcare and life sciences, oil and gas, etc.) or in a geographical location that interests you prior to even starting your MBA. You can find people to get in touch with through your undergraduate alumni database, LinkedIn, company websites and HR contacts, and you can even ask your future MBA program for alumni to speak with. Most people love to talk about themselves and help fellow or future alumni, so while these people are pretty busy, you should be able to find a few that are willing to talk with you. Just make sure that this early in the stage you keep things very broad; do not send them your résumé and do not ask for a job or an interview. Just let them know that you are about to start your MBA, are very interested in their industry and company, and would like to speak to them to learn more about their company, their job, the experience that they've had working in both, and to get any advice that they can offer. Most companies will appreciate the initiative early on and it may give you a leg up in the process. A lot of people do not think to begin doing this so early; however, it really can't do you any harm, unless of course you make an ass out of yourself on your informational phone calls or forget to call in.

Everything mentioned above is also true once you are already a student and are formally going through the recruiting process. Make sure to try and network and speak with as many people as you can. Not only will this get you on your target company's radar, but it will also allow you to learn more about the company and the type of work that you could potentially be doing. This is great to know and helpful when it comes to being prepared for the interview process, or maybe to help you realize that you might want to consider a different company or line of work.

I'm actually on the receiving end of a lot of these networking/informational interview calls these days, because I am active in heading up MBA recruiting from my alma mater at my company. I'm not in HR or a full-time recruiter, but I work with them a lot as part of the "extracurricular" stuff that I do in addition to my full-time role. You'll learn later on that all the networking and extracurricular stuff never really ends, even when you're out of school.

One of the gentlemen that I met while back on campus at a recruiting event wanted to set up a networking/informational interview call. No problem, happy to speak to any interested students. On paper he looked like a great candidate; however, the conversation at the campus event seemed scripted in a very obvious way. I felt like I was speaking with any number of sci-fi movie robots from the 80s or 90s. He called me on time (good start), but told me about five minutes into the call that he needed to call me back in a few minutes because he had a family emergency that he needed to deal with. No problem, definitely more important than whatever bullshit we were about to talk about! After he called me back a few minutes later, he went on to tell me that apparently he and his mom had very different ideas of an emergency, and that she was in a department store shopping for him and wanted to know his size and what color polo shirts he already had. I needed to hand it to him, he at least had somewhat of a sense of humor about it, but it was probably not the best idea to tell me all of those details that are hilarious for me and likely embarrassing as hell for him.

Another guy that I was supposed to have some networking calls with actually seemed like a pretty good candidate. He definitely had the background and education for some of the roles that we recruit for, and I had met and spoken with him at a few of our recruiting events. All of the conversations went well, he asked great questions, and he seemed knowledgeable about the industry and the company. He reached out to me via email and wanted to set something up, so we did. One little problem though, the call never came! I double-checked emails about the date, the time, that he had my number and understood that he was to call me -- no issues there. I didn't hear anything from him all night. I generally do these calls in the evenings after my work hours, so I do plan my evening somewhat to make sure I have time to talk and am at home or in a quiet place. As you can imagine, I don't like trying to help people out only to have them waste my time. I found out the next day (only because I reached out to him first) that he also had a family emergency and was flying during our call. True or not, I understand completely and looked to set up another call with him. This time he *did* call -- except he called 3 hours late, at 10pm! I just let it go to voicemail, having decided I was not going to waste my time with this guy anymore. He never explained why he was late, followed up with an email, or anything like that. In either case, I made it clear I wasn't going to schedule another call. I actually will be on campus for first-round interviews and will be having the pleasure of interviewing this guy tomorrow, so I'm pretty curious to see how that goes. Assuming he actually shows up and is on time, of course. Remember to have some common courtesy, be on time for your calls and realize that it isn't an alum's job to talk to you, so they're likely taking time out of their schedule and doing you a favor. Don't make them regret that or remember you for the wrong reasons.

Job and Formal Interviews:

Job interviews are a little bit different from informational and networking interviews. I have gone through the recruiting process on both ends of the table for both finance and strategy roles, but this should all be good for any type of interview.

Let's start with the basics that you'll probably regret spending money on this book to hear, because I'm talking to you like a child and it's all common sense. But believe me, I'm writing this because as obvious as it is, you wouldn't believe how many people botch this. Be on time. Be dressed appropriately -- considering that you are getting your MBA and likely not applying for a job as a roughneck on an oil rig, this means business professional attire. Bring copies of your résumé. Your interviewer will already have it with them, but it is a good idea to bring one and it shows that you pay attention to detail. Also, sometimes the formatting that comes out of the computer submissions systems gets skewed, so this will show that you actually do know how to use Word and can proofread things.

Speaking of your résumé, this is something that you should know inside and out. If you're asked to walk through your résumé or any specifics that are mentioned on it, you shouldn't need to look at it or use it as a reference. It's a document about you, written by you; know it backwards and forwards! While this should be common sense, I did interview someone that initially looked to be an awesome candidate on paper, who clearly needs this advice and didn't get the memo. While answering every single question that involved either his background or past work experience, the dude would literally look straight down at his résumé and some other sheet that looked like it had typed responses on it. While I will discuss interview prep in this section, do *not* bring your damn prep paper to the interview and read your responses off of it! It was almost as if this was some random guy filling in for who I thought I was interviewing and he was just reading about the dude for the first time. Overall, it was pretty strange, and definitely not impressive. If he had been sitting in a dunk tank or over a trap door, I would've hit the drop button well before the interview ended.

I won't go into detail or dedicate a section to how to write your résumé since your school should have dedicated staff to help out with that, but I will say to not be lazy and make sure you spend some time in tailoring your résumé to the specific company or jobs that you are applying to. Your résumé is not a one-size-fits-all type of deal; customize it for the different jobs that you're applying to. For example, if you are interested in a finance career, it may not make a whole lot of sense to list your memberships in the dozen clubs you are likely a member of in school (marketing, operations, etc.). It's great to be an involved student, but don't put down any red flags that make people question if you really do want a career in finance (or whatever your chosen field is). On a similar note, you will likely only have space for two to four bullets per job, depending on how many jobs you have had that are relevant to list. You should craft each bullet point to be a fit for the types of roles that you are applying for, and should make sure that you have a good mix of skills represented by your different bullet points. You may very well have two different resumes with entirely different bullet points for different types of functional fields that you are targeting, such as consulting and finance. This is one of those areas where it will pay off to put in a little bit of extra effort.

The main things you need to work on are company prep, industry prep, and general interview prep. Let's start with general interview prep since this will apply to any interview. You need to be prepared for and expect a wide range of behavioral and situational interview questions, as well as some technical and case related questions.

For the behavioral and situational questions, I'm talking about the kind that typically starts off with, "Tell me about a time when…" Your program will likely have a whole list of these questions for you to review, so do just that! Know your stories and work experience that apply to a lot of the generic questions that are typically asked about leadership, team work, tight deadlines, going along with an idea you don't agree with, a time you took initiative, improved a process, etc. When you answer these questions, try to use the STAR format.

I know, this sounds cheesy as hell, but it helps get your point across and is a great way to organize your thoughts. As an interviewer I get seriously frustrated when the interviewee answers questions in a way that is fragmented and hard to follow, and sometimes they take tangents that don't even answer the initial questions. The **STAR** format is basically just a way to set up and answer the questions. You start by providing background and explaining the **Situation**, then talk about your **Task** at hand, the **Action** that you took, and the **Result**. If you can throw in any type of lesson learned at the end, then even better.

When answering the situational and behavioral questions, try to draw on different experiences. One thing that employers can't get enough of is someone with a diverse background and different sets of experiences and skills. Even if you have had the same job for the entire time between undergrad and grad school, it's no excuse to be a one-trick pony when it comes to the interview. You can use classroom and academic situations as examples, as well as something from your personal life. I've had someone use their training for the Olympics as a way to address adversity, hardship, and dedication and another person use being a junior Martial Arts instructor in an academy full of very experienced and older instructors as the basis for a story of how he handles being a mediator and is able to influence others that may not be open to his point of view. Both ended up being great ways to address the question at hand. One of them received a full-time job offer and the other has just recently earned a summer job

As much as interviewers love to hear about diverse experiences, they don't like to hear the same thing over and over again. I had one candidate not only use the same job for three or four responses back to back, but he used the same project! Yes, the new reporting that you created for your business unit sounds like a fantastic project, learning experience, and good result. Okay, yes, I heard about that, I get it, great job. Okay...seriously, again? Is this the only accomplishment you've ever had in your life, or the only thing that you did in that job over the course of three years? Whether the story can be adapted to answer every question in an interview or not, it doesn't mean that it should be! Don't just tell potential employers about how diverse you are in your cover letter, especially because they don't read those anyways, but rather show them in the interview.

Case and technical interview questions are best prepared for through practice. You obviously will not know what type of questions will be asked exactly, but if you can answer with an easy to follow and logical thought process, then it will be a job well done. Be able to do some quick math in your head or written out; practicing this ahead of time may seem silly but can help get your mind in the right gear. For the case questions, work with your consulting club and career services center to get specific examples to practice through or recommendations for books that are devoted solely to that topic. What I can tell you though is to practice those cases as if you were in a real interview. Write out your responses, talk through your thought process, and make sure to ask the interviewer plenty of clarifying questions or for data that would be helpful to you that they did not provide in the initial prompt. You don't need to get the exact answer to these questions, and depending on what the case is there may not even be an exact answer. What the interviewers are looking for is that you can organize your thoughts in a logical way, sort through what is and what is not important data, ask appropriate questions, and come up with a logical, rationale recommendation or response.

Company and industry prep are very important when it comes to these interviews as well. While you will likely not get many targeted, specific questions that can be answered by this type of preparation, it will allow you to ask well thought out questions and to carry on a general conversation about the company or industry that if you have trouble doing will be a huge red flag. We had one girl that was interviewing for a Strategy role with us and pretty much had the offer in the bag until one of our executives asked her a fairly broad question about a large acquisition that we recently made. The girl was clueless that the acquisition even took place and the executive recommended to not move forward with her at all. Do your homework! Read up on public filings and news stories on the company to learn how they are doing financially, about any acquisitions or divestitures they may have made recently, and to get a sense of what their main strategic priorities and business models are. For the industry side of things, look to see if there have been any mergers or acquisitions in the industry, any new regulations that may affect current business models, etc. Make sure you ask questions based on the research that you did or bring it up in responses to other questions to show the interviewers that you truly are interested in their company and industry.

Pre-interview Dinners:

This is one category that you may not encounter before every interview, but you will certainly encounter plenty of these in your life. For on-campus interviews, you may have a recruiting dinner the night before with all of the interviewers that are in town from the company along with the other candidates. For second or final-round interviews that are often on-site with the companies, you may have this dinner with the next day's interviewers or even senior leaders and other managers within the organization, along with other former interns and recent MBA hires. My best advice for these events is to be prepared for anything and have all of your interview prep done beforehand. Some of these can be extremely casual, get-to-know-you type events, whereas others may have an element of an interview and evaluation thrown in. Also, the experience can vary widely depending on where you are sitting. You may literally be sitting next to the CEO or CFO that grills you in a somewhat playful way on facts about their company, or you may sit next to someone like me, who is perfectly content to talk about the city, what I like to do on the weekend, or pretty much anything else that's on your mind. No matter what the atmosphere feels like, make no mistake about it, you *are* being judged and evaluated on how you interact with people in a more casual setting, so try not to get too casual and talk about going out to the bars every weekend or crazy stories that aren't exactly work-appropriate.

The best way to prepare for these dinners (aside from the interview prep that should've occurred beforehand) is to come prepared with a lot of questions fitting for a dinner like this, such as what it's like to work at the company, what there is to do around the city (assuming it is not in your hometown or where your school is located), what the people you're speaking with like to do in their spare time, etc. Aside from all of that, I'll just give you a few examples of ways that you could be put on the spot. Our CFO *loves* to put people in the hot seat at larger meetings. He does not discriminate; he will do it to the whole room when he has the chance at any type of event, be it a recruiting dinner, a management training program meeting, etc.

I recently had the pleasure of attending one of these dinners for our MBA recruits that were in town to interview the next day. I was not interviewing the next day, but I do attend all the recruiting events and took part in first-round interviews on campus, so I get to come to all of the other recruiting events that are part of the process. After the first-round interviews, our Treasurer (who was also an interviewer for our first-round interviews) sent a question around, asking: If you were making the decision at our company and had $350M cash to use on one single acquisition, what would it be and why? Everyone sent their responses in and probably thought that was the last they'd hear of that question. Wrong! Our CFO mentioned at the dinner that he had just read the responses and wanted to go around the table, giving everyone thirty seconds to pitch their acquisition company to us. Keep in mind that this is a large Fortune 500 company and at the dinner are the CFO, the Treasurer, and the head of Strategy &

Corporate Development, as well as several other SVPs, VPs, Directors, and me, the lowly Manager. I think it's fair to say that this was probably a pretty damn intimidating group to the candidates. Before the first candidate started, our CFO looked at me and nodded at my watch, saying, "You keep time!" So, the first girl started to stammer out a response and as thirty seconds ran out, I gave the nod and our CFO said, "Eerrrrrr!!! NEXT!" And so this went for the first few people. You'd be surprised how good the rest of the group became at self-policing in regards to the thirty seconds after the first couple of candidates literally had the buzzer yelled in their face as they were cut off from making their pitch. We had a couple of international recruits that seemed to struggle to even say hello in English, so I felt bad and overlooked the clock; they may have gotten a minute or so each. No matter what, come prepared for anything and the different types of characters that you are bound to meet at these events. Be ready to think on your feet and hopefully to have people remember you for a good idea or response as opposed to being the one that got tongue-tied with a deer-in-the-headlights look on their face.

I was actually placed at the table one person away from our CFO, who was at the head. This was a long table and a big group (over twenty people), so he basically was only able to talk to me and the 3 candidates nearby for most of the night. I guess he got bored at some point, because he started firing off company-related questions and going around the three to see if they could answer. "Who is our Chief Investment Officer?" After a minute of crickets...drum roll and the answer is...we don't have one. Trick question. "How many people work for us total?" "What's our CEOs name?" Mostly simple stuff that is found on our website.

Then he asked, "So what's our company's market cap?" If you don't know this, it is simply the market price of your stock per share, multiplied by your number of shares outstanding. Any market screen (Yahoo, Google, CNBC, you name it) on the company ticker will list this along with a fifty-two-year high/low, etc. He also wasn't letting me off the hook on this one. Not only should I know this because I work in finance, but I work in Treasury at that! I actually didn't know the exact number because our stock price had had a good run as of late and the market cap had gone up a bit, so I told him I could give him a ballpark figure after we heard what the recruits could come up with. This is where it got a little embarrassing. The first girl started off, "Okay, well, you have $X amount in revenue, $X amount in earnings, so the answer is $X."

Our CFO was nodding and playing along, while I could see the evil glint light up in his eye as he responded, "Okay, great...so what's our market cap?" Clearly she wasn't getting it. Neither was the next guy. He grasped at straws and after a few awkward seconds of some hems and haws, he blurted out a percentage. Wrong! Market cap is a dollar value, not a percentage! Okay, next. The girl had no idea, but at least she admitted that she didn't know what the market cap was. I gave an answer that was within about 10%, admitting that I knew it wasn't exact but was close.

Want to know what the recruits did wrong here? Besides the easier-to-overlook transgression of not knowing what the actual market cap was, it was pretty clear that they had no clue what market cap even means! Market cap is not a percentage and has nothing to do with your revenue, or your earnings, for that matter. If you are in MBA-level interviews, whether for finance, strategy, or any other function (these folks were interviewing for finance and strategy) please have a clue what some basic financial metrics are and where the company that you are interviewing with stands. If you don't know something, it is all right to admit that and try to come up with a best or reasonable guess. If these recruits had asked some clarifying questions or admitted to not knowing up front, they wouldn't have looked like idiots for clearly trying to make stuff up. When you're speaking with the CFO, you aren't going to be able to bullshit him on what something that he asks you about is, so don't make it up and save some face here.

Career Fairs:

Believe it or not, one huge part of both internship and full-time recruiting is the career fair, and this is the perfect environment to show off your skills in all of the other mentioned areas of this section, as you will likely have the chance to interview, attend a dinner event, and most certainly network with recruiters! The fairs can vary greatly in terms of size, length, types of companies, etc. There are two massive career fairs put on every year by different minority organizations (NBMBAA – National Black MBA Association and

NSHMBA – National Society of Hispanic MBAs) but have no fear if you are plain ol' white folk like myself, because these events really are for everyone to attend, and everyone does. These two fairs are multiple-day events and they are huge, like entirely-fill-up-some-of-the-largest-convention-centers-in-the-country huge. These are worth attending even though you will most likely have some travel expenses related with doing so. Hey, you have to spend money to make money, right? There will also be smaller, more local or regional fairs, as well as some small niche ones (specifically health care-related or the like). Your MBA program may also reimburse you up to a set amount (I believe ours was $300 or $500) per year to use for job search-related travel or career fair attendance.

The approach for the career fair is to really be prepared for anything. You need to do some work ahead of time if you really want to get the most out of this. For the larger fairs, you'll be able to apply for specific jobs online ahead of time and be able to interview with the companies directly at the fair if they want to meet with you. Make sure that you apply before the résumé drop deadlines, otherwise you likely won't be able to get a spot. If you do end up getting an interview slot with some companies that are at the fairs, you may get invited to some of those sweet dinner events that I told you about earlier. If you don't end up getting an interview slot, don't fret. Some companies will actually grant and give interviews on the spot if they like you! The way it works at the larger fairs, people lamely wait in line, sometimes for quite a while (Deloitte and some of the larger, well-known companies tend to get lines eerily similar to the ones outside the Apple store whenever a new iPhone comes out) to speak to recruiters and give them their thirty-second elevator pitch about why they are a great candidate and then spend the rest of the time basically kissing ass about how awesome the company is and why they want to work there. If you do a really good job at kissing the recruiter's ass, then they may just pull you back into a little room they have set up behind their table and go through a quick first-round interview. Just like that! So, even if you don't have anything on the books ahead of the trip, definitely do your interview prep and be ready for anything.

For the larger career fairs, you need to have a game plan, not just walk around aimlessly and randomly stop by booths of companies that look cool or that you actually recognize the name of. Review the list of attending companies beforehand and decide which ones you want to speak with, so that you can do some research ahead of time. Remember that these recruiters will literally meet hundreds of candidates in a short amount of time. If you just show up and aren't up to date on the company and industry background or able to speak to them intelligently, and instead just ask the same generic questions that you ask every other company and that they likely hear from a majority of the other candidates, then they will not remember you. Your résumé will be callously thrown on the pile of the ones that they'll later use as toilet paper. You don't want your résumé to end up on the toilet paper pile. To the same end, try to get a card or contact info from the recruiters so that you can follow up with them later, particularly shortly after the career fair to keep the dialogue going. I've always found it invaluable to have a real, live contact at the company that you can speak with and get in front of during the recruiting process, as opposed to just facelessly submitting a cover letter and résumé online and quickly getting lost in the tidal wave of résumés that the company is likely receiving during a normal recruiting period. They're also a great opportunity to get tons of free stuff! Be shameless and go talk to some crappy company that you've never heard of or have no interest in working for if it means you can snag some cool stuff gratis from their recruiters! Trust me, they don't mind. When I am in their position I prefer that people come take all of the crap we're giving away off of the table, otherwise it means I need to deal with packing it up and shipping it back to corporate.

Info Sessions:

One of the best things about being an MBA student at a top school is all of the recruiting opportunities that you don't need to travel or go out of your way for; with Informational Sessions (Info Sessions) being the main format. An info session is pretty much what it sounds like. Companies come on campus and will have generally an hour-long session (sometimes followed by a networking session) where they basically pitch you on why their company is awesome to work for. The time is normally evenly split between their presentation and when they open the floor up for Q&A.

You don't need much specific advice for the Q&A piece since everything that I have already discussed in prior sections is relevant. However, do your research to make sure you know the company and the industry, don't ask bullshit questions that they know you don't care about the answer to, and don't ask questions that you can easily find the answer to on their website or with a two-second Google search. *Do* ask questions that are interesting, insightful, or about some piece of company or industry news that is recent and relevant. Asking the speaker about their personal experience and career path is fair game as well, and you'll soon learn that people love to talk about themselves.

During recruiting season you will likely have tons of info sessions that you can attend -- so many that oftentimes you will want to say, "Screw this, I'd much rather spend an hour in the evening after classes drinking with my friends." or catching up on work for your classes or spending time with your family, if that's more your speed. If you think that there is even a remote possibility of you applying to this company in the future, suck it up and attend the session. Believe it or not, sitting in the back and not asking any questions is still better than not showing up at all. You might actually learn something that you can use later, but the main reason is that companies do track attendance at all of their on-campus and career fair events. However, it won't exactly look great if you show up to all four events a company may have on campus but you don't speak to anyone and nobody can remember who the hell you are when they see you pop up so frequently in their attendance-tracking file. Think of it this way: if you're a recruiter and someone is telling you in their cover letter (which wouldn't matter since those almost always instantaneously go the recruiter's toilet paper pile before being read) or during a first-round interview how much they love your company and want to work there, you're going to have a hard time believing that if you check the attendance list for the three recruiting events you did at their school that year and they couldn't even drag their ass to one of them. Normally these attendance lists are checked even before getting to the interview stage, as it comes into play as a factor to consider when you are reviewing résumés to see who you want to even interview in the first place. Guess what -- students that have attended events and had some type of dialogue with recruiters will absolutely have a leg up here.

One other and very important reason to attend some of these events is the food. Yes, there is often times free catering brought in! This may not sound like a big deal to you now, but as you will once again learn in the position of a starving and broke student, a free meal is monumental. I've had everything from pizza to barbeque and even sushi at these events, and it all tasted even more delicious since it wasn't on my dime! Also, occasionally there will be beer and wine to complement whatever food or snacks they bring in. Sounds like a no-brainer when it comes to attending these things, doesn't it?

However, don't attend these events and call attention to yourself for being a mooch. At one event that I put on as part of my MBA recruiting activities in my current job (as opposed to one that I attended as a student), were myself, someone from the company that actually works full time as a recruiter for college relations, and our Treasurer. My entire role at this event was to stand in the corner the whole time and smile and nod while the Treasurer was giving the presentation, and to smile and nod extra hard and enthusiastically when he pointed to me as the recent alumnus who did an internship at the company and is now loving life, having made the decision to come back and work for them full time. Of course, I also networked with students and answered some questions for them in discussion after the presentation.

Anyways, we decided to be gracious hosts and cater food in for this event. We wanted to do something a little different, so we decided to get some good, local barbeque. I mean, who doesn't like some good barbeque, right? If you are thinking to yourself that you don't, please write me with your name and address. I'll make sure to visit you so that I can ring your doorbell and slap you in the face with a tasty pulled pork sandwich once you answer. As luck would have it, our food was late. This created quite a commotion, as we had a few trays of food set up at the front of the room while our Treasurer was going through the company spiel. Everyone just sat there awkwardly staring at it at first, not wanting to be rude to the Treasurer, but clearly foaming at the mouth with anticipation of getting their hands on some delicious barbeque to help soothe the pain of trying to stay awake while someone pitches them on yet another awesome company to work at.

Our Treasurer said, "Hey guys, we have all of this food here for you. No worries, don't be shy, please help yourself." Well, a few awkward minutes later and someone finally said to themselves, I would imagine, "Damn it, I'm hungry." They got up and of course everyone else followed suit. While this was a minor disturbance, I wouldn't say it was a big deal until one of the biggest clusterfucks of recruiting history ever took place. Someone had moved one of the meat trays so that a good portion of it was hanging off the ledge of the table that it was on. The room had stadium seating with the food set up towards the top near the entrance; that way the caterers made a little less of a distraction while setting up. However, now one of the trays had been moved by someone to the point of almost teetering off the ledge -- pretty much a ticking time bomb.

Someone was a little overzealous and jammed their tongs down into the tray, thinking to themselves, "Man, this is going to be awesome!" and let me tell you folks, it *was* awesome. Not the food that the student thought he was going to eat, but the fact that he didn't realize the tray was hanging halfway off the table and he jammed the tongs down to the wrong end. He basically see-sawed the whole tray over, and there ended up being about 5 pounds of dripping wet barbeque meat flying through the air. Luckily the Treasurer and I were better protected than most Presidents, having a sea of black suits between us and the dangerous, flying projectiles. The students in the black suits weren't quite as fortunate. They were sitting lower than the table due to the stadium seating and in a perfect position to be covered in barbeque sauce and meat. It was everywhere, and no doubt ruined what may have been their only interview suits. Well kiddos, looks like it's time to take a field trip to Macy's this weekend!

I about lost my shit and it took every ounce of strength In me to not fall down to the floor and roll around in some type of hysterical fit laughing. Instead I said I was going to run out and grab some stuff to clean it up, at which point I then left the room and had my hysterical fit. Talk about interrupting a presentation! Our Treasurer actually kept his cool and paused for a minute, then just kept going on with the presentation while trying to ignore the clean-up. The funniest part is that the student who knocked it over said he was going to run out to grab some cleaning supplies as well, except he never came back! I can only imagine he instead had to run to the bathroom to clean the skid marks that must've materialized in his pants after pulling a blunder like that.

<u>Student Life</u>

This is probably one of the areas that you're most interested in -- learning about what your life will be like for the next 21 months or so. Well, let me tell you, it is likely going to be very different than what you initially imagined and will most certainly be worlds apart from your undergraduate experience. There's a lot to discuss here, some more important than the rest, but I'll try to paint as clear a picture as possible in regards to both the social and academic aspects of student life.

The Characters You'll Meet:

I think the title of this section says it all, as well as the fact that I am devoting an entire section to this topic. You are about to enter a very unique social ecosystem that will contain even more unique inhabitants. As mentioned earlier, I was in a program that was toward the smaller to middle class size among other top 25 programs, but even if you are in a smaller program, expect to see the same type of diversity that I did.

Welcome to the fishbowl. A graduate MBA program is actually like a time warp or some type of social retardation where you end up in an environment much like that in middle or high school. Everyone will be in your business, and everyone will talk to others about your business, whether what they are saying is true or not. Sad as it is, this is kind of inevitable unless you withdraw from social events almost entirely. But where's the fun in that? Just remember that you're in a program with a lot of other smart and motivated individuals, but that we're all motivated by different things. People will care about and talk about your social life because they want to make themselves feel better or look better, because they feel threatened by you, because they just like to gossip, want to be alpha male or queen bitch of the pack, etc. I'm just letting you know this as a word of warning in case you want to keep your life private or don't want to get caught up in teenage-like social politics.

Your classmates will likely be from all over the world geographically and all walks of life both culturally and in regards to their past work experience. You'll have people with little to no work experience at all (although not many will fall into this category), people who have been investment bankers, entrepreneurs, military pilots or infantrymen, and everything in between. You'll have people who are super-focused on grades and the job search, and others who couldn't care less for any number of reasons but really just want to go out and get wasted every night. There will be single people, married people, people with families, and people that are married and/or have families but act single. I always found it kind of sad when everyone knew who the married people were sleeping with, yet you occasionally saw their spouse at some school function or event and they just seemed completely clueless. I am not the cheating type myself, so I don't quite understand the phenomenon, but you'll definitely get a glimpse into what motivates other people. You'll have all types of people from all walks of life to deal with in your program.

Student Clubs:

As you can imagine, there are tons of options for student clubs. Most will be career-oriented (Oil & Gas Industry Club, Finance Club, Consulting Club, etc.) but others will be entirely social (Extreme Sports Club, Beer and Wine Club, etc.). You definitely need to be in clubs, at least from the career-search standpoint, if only to be able to list them on your résumé. Most clubs will have some type of annual fee, but it is worth it. Just make sure to attend some of the lunch events or end-of-year club parties to make sure to get your money's worth of food and booze!

Even if you think you know exactly what you want to do early on, I still recommend joining some clubs that are adjacent or even entirely outside of whatever that functional area is. You'll be surprised about the overlap, or how things that you do in one functional club can be adapted to answer interview questions for a completely different functional area's job interview. Also, they all can have some pretty cool events that you might want to take advantage of and use to network with other people in your program. One thing to remember though: just because you might be in six to eight different clubs, it likely doesn't make sense to list them all on your résumé! Adapt your résumé for each job that you're applying to, to list only the relevant clubs. If possible, try to get involved to the point where you have a leadership position. Most of these positions are elected, and that goes a long way toward showing recruiters that you can influence and lead people, and you'll likely have some great projects or situations to talk about with them as a result of that leadership position. Just remember that if you actually *do* get elected to a position, you likely won't have the joy of only being involved to the point of paying your dues, showing up for free food, and listing it on your résumé. You may actually have some real work to do!

One other idea for you to play with is that the possibility of creating your own club is always there. If there is a specific industry that you are interested in that is not represented by another club, or even some type of social thing you like to do, definitely see if there is enough interest to form a club. For example, if you know you want to work in the Oil and Gas Industry (which isn't a bad idea if you're looking for a corporate gig, they pay nice salaries and fat bonuses) but there isn't a strong on-campus recruiting presence from those companies or a related club, start one up! This could be enough to start to bring some of those companies on campus, and it's definitely a way for you to get a foot in the door. This normally opens you up to some type of school funding for the club each year, and again is a great way to show companies that you are willing and able to take initiative and lead people. I know I mentioned this before, but this is kind of a key theme when it comes to the job search at the management level: you need to be able to show how you've done things, not just be able to talk about how you can or why you can. Results speak louder than words.

Remember when I mentioned that you may get some school funds for the club? You can likely use them to organize a trip out to Houston (the mecca for US headquarters of all the big Oil and Gas companies) to meet with some of the large players in the industry. If there are certain companies that you want to target that don't target your school, you should look for ways to go to them. Organizing a group of other interested students and setting up an informational on-site visit with the company will be something that most are more than open to, and it should be well received by them. We had a group of students do that recently for my company even though we recruited on campus at their school. Talk about initiative! It should be no surprise that I recognized many faces from that group when it came time to go through second-round interviews back at Corporate and even now into the summer, as a few of them converted their interviews into internships.

When it comes to clubs, try to be strategic about what you do attend, and don't attend for the clubs that you're in. Don't think you need to attend everything on the calendar, so go to what makes sense, as you will see a lot of the regular monthly (or weekly, or whatever) meetings can be pretty pointless. Your time will be precious, as you will quickly learn, and you need to defend it tenaciously.

Miscellaneous Events:

On top of all of the recruiting-focused and club events on your calendar, there will be tons of other events to go around. Miscellaneous events is a pretty generic title, but most of these will end up in what can be called the "shit show" events category. Luckily my program (and likely yours as well) had a regularly-scheduled weekly shit show event! We had a built-in happy hour where every Thursday after classes ended for the week (we didn't have classes on Friday), there would be several kegs brought into the business school lobby. Some weeks there would be special events wrapped up with the happy hour event, like the international food fair or marketing competition, whereas other weeks there was no thin veil of academia or cultural awareness and it was just about blowing off some steam and free beer!

Regardless if it is just a happy hour or some other type of combined event, it will likely be fun and you will see some funny stuff. Like the one (or several) creepy guy(s) in your class that date undergrads and think they're super-cool for sneaking in their underage girlfriend for a drink, even when there's no "sneaking in" since nobody checks ID's or really cares. Even funnier, during the marketing competition event, we had a large pet food company as one of the sponsors. The competition was laid out where companies sponsored a group of students to help showcase their products and services at a marketing booth that they set up, with the attending students all voting on which group did the best job. Well, tons of students brought their dogs in for this event since there was a "Cutest Pet" contest at the pet food booth, and one of our

Vietnamese classmates thought it was great, trying to be nice to the dogs and play with them in the lobby. Funny thing is the dogs weren't having it. They were friendly as hell to the dozens of other people there, but all treated this chick as if she was trying to steal their food. They all started barking and going crazy around her; were they racist? I don't know, but it did bring to mind how she was telling me just the week before how they eat dogs in Vietnam, and that she particularly likes to eat dog testicles. I think these pooches could sense their fallen comrades on her breath, and were not happy about it!

If your school has something along these lines, my advice is to get your work done for the day beforehand. I can tell you and I'm sure you can imagine, but it is pretty damn hard to have project meetings or wrap up some finance problem sets when you hear music bumping down in the lobby and know that there's free, all-you-can-drink ice cold beer just waiting for you to help kick your weekend off right. Be forewarned though, whenever you attend one of these you will almost always be faced with the devastatingly hard decision between being responsible and going home after a few beers to get some stuff done, or to going out with your buddies and not remembering what the hell happened the night before.

Another category of miscellaneous, high-likelihood-of-turning-into-a-shit-show event would be the tailgate. Ah yes, the ever-loved football tailgate. American academia at its finest! My MBA tailgates were certainly not nearly as rowdy as my undergrad tailgates; I attribute this mostly to the contrast of the size of the school and caliber of football played at each. My undergrad university was about four times larger than the university I attended for my MBA, with the contrast in athletic ability being similar to that noticed when NHL players leave the ice at the end of the period and then the elementary-school-aged peewee team takes the ice to give you something to laugh at between periods. One leg up that my MBA tailgates did have on my undergrad tailgates were that they were there every game and they were well-funded. You will now have the joy of attending your own well-stocked tailgate as opposed to having to sneak into someone else's or hoping they don't notice you leeching off of their keg.

If you don't care about football, I still suggest you attend at least a few of these. Yet again they are another way to get to know your fellow classmates, and of course see some funny stuff happen every now and then. In fact, I would say a majority of tailgate attendees did not actually attend the game, they either just came for the free booze or to mingle with some other students. You might think that you will just see the people that like to go out and party, but really it will be everyone who comes out of the woodwork for these. I remember seeing tons of families, they just may not stay the whole time and will obviously not be hitting the sauce as hard as everyone else. Also, if this is something that your program does not currently do, why not be the one to look into getting it started? I know our program had this previously, but our student government president definitely made this a top priority of his. What was at first just a couple of kegs and maybe some horseshoes at the early tailgates eventually turned into kegs, hard liquor, food, and a DJ every week with us oftentimes inviting other graduate programs within the school to join in the festivities once our new student president was at the reins. How can you argue against that? Bread and circuses, that's all the people want!

Other than the regular happy hour and tailgate events, the other main school-associated event that is for everyone and not recruiting or club affiliated is, of course, the holiday parties. While I must admit I did not attend every one of these (sometimes the tickets were expensive or I had better things to do), I did go to most of them. These are where people really let their guard down and have some fun, sometimes too much fun. I've seen married or engaged people uninhibitedly making out with single students at the bar in front of everyone, other people dancing on top of the bars, all types of shenanigans. We were not allowed back at some venues after our parties, and I remember the outrage that we all felt after the parties later in the year were no longer open bar but instead came with a limited number of drink tickets until it turned into a cash bar. How dare they try to tame us!

One event worth mentioning was our Halloween party. Every year the school sponsored a Halloween party at some local bar and they normally made for a pretty good time. Some buddies and I went to one of those giant costume warehouses and for some strange reason one of the guys was fascinated with this pharaoh costume. He was from Venezuela and we all affectionately called him Hot Dog. To be fair, this was a preexisting nickname that he told us he acquired due to his affection with the Venezuelan street version during his undergrad days. Hot Dog fell in love with this weird pharaoh costume that was pretty much just a long, cult-like dress. He didn't want to hear anything from us about how dumb he looked and even stepped it up by having one of our friends come by and do her best Hollywood stylist job and put eyeliner and makeup on him. I think he just wanted to wear makeup and a dress.

Academics

Classes/Majors:

When it comes to picking a major, I would hope that you have an idea of what type of work you want to do after graduation. There is certainly value in trying to do more than one if possible. I did a double major for my MBA, focusing on two fields with a lot of overlap, both of which I am interested in (Finance and Strategy). Some MBA programs will not let you even pick a major or focus and just offer general MBAs, so this may not even be a choice for some of you.

When it comes to classes, in my mind there are a few that you should take no matter what your focus is. Regardless of if you are going into finance or something a little less technical like HR, take an Excel skills class early on in your MBA if there is one available. This will be an invaluable skill to have while going through your program and will also serve you well once you graduate and start working, regardless of what you're doing. I always thought that I was pretty sufficient in Excel, but taking an Excel-based class really showed me how naïve I was. If you too think you are an Excel expert, you probably just need somebody to come by, pat you on your head, and say, "Bless your heart."

Regardless of what your focus is, you will obviously have to take classes that cover all fields and functions, even if it is just one or two requirements. In addition to the Excel class previously mentioned, look to take some additional HR classes that seem interesting to you. Being a finance and technical guy I always thought of HR as somewhat of a joke, but HR at the MBA level really comes down to organizational design, behavior, and strategy. Not only can it be really interesting to learn about, but it will be good to have some classes under your belt as you progress in your career and actually start to manage some sizeable teams. One of the common things that I hear executives mention in response to being asked to look back at their MBA experience is that they all wished they had taken more HR-based classes. Thinking about it now, I'm not shocked at that response, but it is eerily odd that on several occasions I have heard some pretty senior executives answer exactly the same way, as if they're all reading from the same teleprompter. Aside from HR, look to take a negotiations class if possible. Whether or not you need this for work, it will certainly help you when it comes to negotiating on your own behalf.

In a nutshell, try to take classes that cover two things: what you will need to know for the type of work that you are looking to do, and things that interest you. Hopefully the two will be one and the same, but really try to use this time to learn as much as you can. I remember picking classes during undergrad with zero thought other than "How does this impact how late I can sleep?", "How easy will it be?", and "Do I really need to show up?" You're likely paying a lot for your MBA, so try to milk it for what you can. Don't just take classes because you know they will be easy, in fact you should look to do the opposite and take classes that you know may be a challenge. This is where you will get to focus on building out a weaker skillset or developmental area of yours, or even learning a new one altogether.

Grades:

There will be some people in your program that never take their faces out of their books for enough time to know what month of the year it is, let alone the day of the week. There will also be people that don't care whatsoever about grades. And then there should be you, hopefully falling gracefully somewhere in the middle. The truth of the matter is that your grades don't matter, as long as they are not atrocious. Hopefully you caught that last caveat there. Try to at least stay in the middle of the pack as far as your class goes. If you are looking to go into investment banking or consulting, then they matter a little more, especially if you are younger and have less work experience. However, they do not matter to the point where you need to be concerned about killing yourself in a couple of classes to ensure that you get a 3.57 overall GPA versus a 3.47. If you can speak well to your work experience and can show that you are smart, then you will be just fine. As mentioned before though, keep in mind what you are looking to do and be truthful with yourself about your experience. If you have zero to two years of post-undergrad work experience, then a strong GPA will be helpful. That being said, there were *tons* of people in my class that landed some pretty high-profile investment banking and consulting gigs without even being in the top 20% of the class, so keep that in mind.

Group Work:

As you probably know, you will have to do tons of group projects over the course of your MBA program. Sometimes you will not get a choice as to your group members, but most of the time you will. However, some programs keep you in the same groups for a majority or even all of the program. Find some good teammates and stick with them if possible for certain classes. This will make your life a lot easier. For me, I ended up doing this for a lot of my finance classes. I found a solid group of guys focusing in finance that were smart, accountable, and didn't like to waste time. This made life so much easier for those classes, since instead of starting off meetings wasting an hour by debating who will do what, what approach should we take, and making sure that everyone else knew what the hell they were doing, we all trusted each other to be smart and quickly chopped up the work.

Don't get me wrong, working with different people and getting different perspectives, ideas, etc. is great and you should make sure that you switch it up a bit. So if you want to work for some large, international companies but you have no international experience, there are likely a ton of international students that would love to have you in their group. This is a great way to get some of that experience working with different cultures and language barriers that you'll be able to speak to in interviews. Just make sure you are strong-willed and don't agree to let the Chinese student with terrible spoken and written English be the final editor of a group paper; probably not the best idea.

Overall, just try to find a balance of working with a good group of people you know while also getting to work with some new faces every once in a while. Make sure that you don't work with people that will hold you hostage every time you have a group meeting, where you end up being stuck in a conference room in the library for four or six hours straight because there are one or two people in your group that cannot agree on the most minor of issues or that need to be there to verbally dictate their edits as the rest of the group does some real work and puts the damn deliverable together. To put it bluntly, there will be some crazy people in your program and people that are straight-up impossible to deal with for no good reason, so my advice is mostly around trying to learn who those people are so that you can stay the hell away from them! Your time will be precious, guard it as if you're trying to recover a fumble on your one yard line.

When it comes to group work, it's especially important to hold people (yourself included) accountable and to keep your word. If you are the one that has agreed to compile and edit a group paper or deliverable before submission, you really don't want to be waiting up until 2am the night before it is due at 8am the next day for your teammates to get their acts together and finally send you their work so that you can only then get going on your piece. To the same tune, if you agree to a deadline with someone else, stick to it. They don't care about what excuses you have or how wasted you decided to get the night before, get your part done on time. There will be a time for peer reviews at the end of the course, and believe me, people will nail you for this stuff.

Case Competitions:

Case competitions: something that you will either love or hate, depending on why you are doing one and, of course, how you end up placing! There are competitions for all types of functions and industries, such as Operations, Consulting, Finance, Healthcare, HR/Human Capital, Technology, Real Estate, etc. The competitions are normally put on by a sponsoring company, MBA program, or club. They can be local and just between teams from your school competing against each other, or they can be on a national scale and you may need to travel for some. Some can even be a mix of the two. Now the fun part, the prizes! You can win anything from a congratulations and some pocket change all the way up to summer internship and some serious dough or some type of scholarship. While all competitions are different, prepare to spend an enormous amount of focus in a pretty compressed amount of time if you do plan on signing up and competing in one.

One of the competitions that I participated in was a Deloitte Strategy & Operations Consulting national competition. They started off by holding local events at several schools, with the winning team from each school going on to the national competition. The winners of the local school-level events received a guaranteed first-round interview for a summer position and a free trip down to Miami, Florida where the national competition was being held. The winners of the national competition received a guaranteed summer internship and some prize money. I don't remember the exact amount, but it was likely $10,000 for the first place team, with second and third receiving a few grand as well. Not too bad, right?

So, why should you do a case competition? One reason would be that you are a masochist and like to inflict pain and stress on yourself. Another might be that you really just want to take a crack at the prize money. Really though, you should be looking to do some competitions as just another way to get some good experience, as you can add these to your résumé under your school and club affiliations if you have any free space. Also, it shows that you truly are interested in whatever given field the competition was in. Lastly, as hinted at by some of the prizes mentioned for the Deloitte competition, it is a great way to get in front of specific employers that you may be interested in. Several people from the winning team from our school that went on to the national Deloitte competition ended up getting summer jobs with them and are now working there full time after graduation. They did not win the final competition, but did win first-round interviews and obviously had left an impression on the judges and recruiters from Deloitte.

As for the stress factor, it will likely depend on how high-profile a competition it is and what your motivations for doing it are. For my Deloitte one, we had a team of four people, one who was a good friend of mine, and two who are both smart guys and mean well, but always carried themselves (and their ideas) with an air of pretentiousness that got under my skin. The competition started off at 3pm or so with the Deloitte representatives emailing all of the competitors the scenario and giving us access to a folder *full* of data files - so much crap that the four of us would not have been able to read or sift through it all before the deliverable was due even if that was all that we focused on. Our solution and presentations were to be ready the next day and sent in by 7am, with presentations to the partners and recruiters who were acting as judges starting at 8am. Can you see where this is heading? Something along the lines of everyone maybe getting three or four hours of sleep at best, yet still needing to look polished and put together for a presentation the next day.

You will probably spend the first couple of hours wrapping your head around the case and deciding what your final deliverable should look like. And once you have everything figured out, guess what? You get another email with some new data, just to throw you off and make you rethink everything that you spent the past few hours working on. As I mentioned before, not only must you be a masochist if you want to do some of these, I can also tell you that the people running these things are definitely sadists! Keep in mind that everyone doing this has a reason for doing it and will not be willing to half-ass this the way that they might for a regular group project or something class-related. They don't have to be doing this, so you can bet your ass that they are in it to win it. This means there will likely be some lively discussions around what the data supports and what is the best strategy to solve the case, let alone how you want the presentation to look! A bunch of type-A personalities in this type of scenario with little time to get things done will make your conference room feel like a pressure cooker.

We stayed on campus wrapping up our case and presentation until around 3:30am or so, which was pretty consistent with a lot of the other teams I spoke with, and had to be back on campus in presentation shape by 8am. I watched a few other presentations after ours (you're allowed to sit in and watch after you present, if you want), and a lot of them had the same issue, which was that they had no time to prep. Many people were just disorganized, sloppy, and staring at their damn slides for the whole presentation. One of the guys in my group and I did a good job, but the other two guys were definitely offenders of all of the above just mentioned. Definitely not the way to impress, but the competitions are designed to do this to most people and let the true cream of the crop shine and stand out to the judges. After the judges decide on the winners, one of them spent time with all of the groups individually to provide some feedback, so you do get some personal development out of the process as well.

After the feedback session and finishing up classes for the day, guess how we really wrapped up the case competition? That's right, with a cocktail reception at a local bar and restaurant paid for by Papa Deloitte! Depending on your intentions and reasons for joining the competition, this is something that you can approach from a couple of different angles. One is that it is another great opportunity to meet with some partners of the company and some other consultants and hiring managers, learn more about the type of work they do, projects they're on, and tell them about yourself. Or, you could take the route of my buddy Nick and some other guys that didn't have working for Deloitte as a goal of theirs, and just do your damnedest to run up the bar tab. While I wouldn't exactly recommend this method, I definitely could see where they were coming from. They had just been put through a brutal process, had no further career aspirations or intentions, and wanted to let loose and get some compensation for their time.

I was one of the few poor bastards that actually thought it would be a good idea to have an internship during the school year in order to get some additional experience and, most importantly, make some cash on the side, so I had to show up a little late. When I arrived it was pretty clear to me who was taking what approach to the event. On one side of the bar you had the Deloitte guys cornered and being barraged with questions by the people who actually wanted to work for them, with Nick and some of the people at the other side of the bar literally pounding down tequila shots and getting absolutely torn up on Deloitte's dime. I think the first words Nick stammered to me when I came over to say hello was, "Man, I'm so fucked up!" as he stumbled to stand up straight and minutes later started to get into a faux wrestling match with another guy from the program that was on his level. Bravo, guys, bravo!

Entrepreneurial opportunities:

One thing you may not realize is that going back to school to get your MBA is an absolutely amazing opportunity to get your feet wet in some entrepreneurial activities. I personally am very entrepreneurial and am always looking to start something up on my own or make a quick buck if I can, so this is something that I took advantage of to the fullest. However, even if you don't have entrepreneurship in your blood, you should branch out and try to get involved in developing either your own idea or helping out someone else you know. Most entrepreneurs are exponentially more successful when they have a great support network in place, so what better place to get the support you need than a school full of hungry, smart students and professors that are willing to let you bend their ear?

Your program likely has some types of incubator programs and grants in place to actually get you small amounts of funding for your idea if you either qualify for them or win some type of competition. For example, our program had funds available for you to work on your idea over the summer instead of taking a traditional internship. I don't remember the exact amounts, but I think it was something along the lines of $10,000 or so for the summer. Not what you would earn during an internship, but pretty solid to help out with your business idea or help pay your bills while you give it a shot.

In addition to the summer funding option, my program also had an entrepreneurship competition where you got to develop your idea and present to a panel of judges, with one of them being the generous and filthy rich benefactor whose funds are the ones being given away. Much like a case study competition, they'll question you on all aspects of your idea and choose a winner to receive the funds, to be disbursed in stages as you develop your business. I don't remember the amount of funding for this exactly, but again I think it was somewhere along the lines of $10-20,000. Not only is this a good way to try and scratch together some seed capital, but it'll focus you not only on developing your idea and building out your business plan, but also putting together a polished investor pitch. I believe a lot of top MBA programs have various funding options and competitions like this, so definitely take advantage of the opportunity while you have it.

One of the best things about starting some type of venture of your own while pursuing your MBA is the free labor and class credit! That's right, you will have a pretty much endless flow of opportunities to have other students work with you on your idea for free; no hourly rate, no equity stake, nothing! I don't want this to come off as me recommending taking advantage of people, because really it is their choice to work with you or not, and I'm sure you'll find out that most are happy to do it if they like you or your idea. A ton of your classes will involve group projects, and a lot of those projects will be up to you to decide what you want to work on -- so have the project be related to your business. This can work for pretty much any class you take that is more of an elective and not a core class, as you normally have more leeway in the electives to pick projects.

It likely will be a given point in any entrepreneurship-oriented class you take that you will be able to work on your own business ideas as opposed to doing typical case studies and more rigid assignments that you may have in some of your other classes. Not everyone in those classes will have their own idea or be serious about starting a business of their own, so you'll have plenty of volunteers to help work on your team for the group work as opposed to trying to come up with something of their own. Believe me, this is huge and will save you a ton of time when it comes to doing market research, putting together financials and marketing plans, and it is always great to have people with different backgrounds and experiences to act as a sounding board for your ideas or business model in general.

You don't necessarily need to be bound by classes to work on your idea and have it contribute toward completing your MBA. Most programs will allow some type of independent study as long as you have it sponsored by a professor that you check in with and have some type of deliverables that the two of you agree on before you start the study. What you'll want to do here is work with the professor that teaches a lot of entrepreneurship or venture capital focused classes and set up an independent study with them.

This is a really good way to free up your class schedule to work on your idea at your own pace and also get credit at the same time. Hard to argue with that!

By now you're probably wondering what my idea was, right? Well, in case you haven't noticed throughout the book so far, I do enjoy a little indulgence of the sauce every once in a while. In fact, I'm pretty sure that if I didn't regularly throw them out, I would've had to wade through empty handle-sized (1.75 Liters for those non-alcoholics reading) bottles of Maker's Mark to get across my small one-bedroom apartment by the end of my first year in grad school. There was my idea. Not an empty-liquor-bottle clean-up service, but a distillery. Small craft distilleries and breweries have been on fire over the past few years, and it can be quite an attractive industry to get into. No, you will not be seeing the types of returns that venture capitalists are interested in seeing, where you are able to cash out after just a few years at a stupidly high multiple, but you can make some good cash flow and have a pretty good life.

One of my good friends, Drew, came to get his MBA with the goal of starting his own brewery, and was an engineer and avid home brewer. Match made in heaven? Yes, which serves to point out that if you can find someone to partner up with, it will be very helpful. Sure, that means more mouths to feed, so to speak, but it is well worth it to get a different point of view, different skill sets, and diverse experiences involved in the project. Besides, this will be an incredibly busy time of your life and you can only be in one place at once.

As you know from my brief intro about myself at the beginning of this book, we did not get a distillery, or the brewery that we ultimately pivoted the idea into and spent the bulk of our time on, off the ground. I do not regret the experience one bit, though, and definitely recommend that you look to get involved in some type of entrepreneurial project regardless of if it gets off of the ground or not. You will learn a lot and hone some crucial skills that you may not otherwise have had a chance to flex, and that will become invaluable in the corporate world, or wherever you ultimately end up working.

After we had some initial talks about our idea and what we wanted to do with the business, we of course had the urge to actually develop a product. Now for those reading, let me just put the disclaimer out there that the rest of these events would be illegal, and therefore of course did not actually happen. In this great country of ours we are allowed to legally brew our own beer and make our own wine, but for some reason liquor is off the table. Makes sense, doesn't it!? Anyways, for anyone who doesn't know how to make whiskey or any other type of liquor, it is pretty much a type of beer wash that is then distilled. In order to make liquor from scratch, you basically need to brew up and ferment some beer, and then distill it. The mix of grains that you use will likely be different than most beers, and you will also not carbonate the beer wash. Luckily, my buddy had a pretty serious homebrew setup; now all we needed was a still.

This is where Jesse James's Monster Garage meets alcoholics meets MBA students. We didn't have the money or desire to order a custom-made still from some yahoo hillbilly somewhere in the mountains of Appalachia, so we decided to build one ourselves. The great thing about Home Depot and Lowe's is that they have pretty much everything you could ever need for most projects around the house, and knowledgeable staff to help you pick out the right stuff. However, it gets interesting when you need to carefully think about the way you phrase your questions so that the dude in plumbing doesn't realize you are going to jerry-rig a copper refrigeration coil to be a key component of a liquor still!

After quite a bit of research and some trial and error, we had our still ready to go. We were going to do a mix of corn, barley, and rye; you can get this at the local homebrew store, but it is pretty expensive and we thought we had a better idea. Tractor Supply! That's right, we went on down to the local tractor supply store and picked up a big 'ole sack of some animal feed that was made up of exactly the right ingredients for us. With the ingredients in hand and the still ready to go, it was time for our first test run. We went back to my buddy's place, broke out his homebrew equipment, and made ourselves some beer wash. After a couple of weeks' fermentation period, it was time to distill. Technically we didn't need the still finished before we made the beer wash, but we wanted to make sure we had everything we needed to

66

get going. One glorious Friday when we had no more classes for the week, I walked over to Drew's place, since he lived about two blocks from me, to finally make some whiskey. Waiting for the beer wash to ferment felt like an eternity!

After I got to Drew's, we went to his second bathroom to pull the five-gallon container holding what was to be our whiskey out of his shower, until it hit us straight in the face -- the smell. What, the hell, is that smell!? We popped the lid off the bucket and it got even more overpowering. Literally, neither of us could breathe without almost throwing up all over the place. Something had gone terribly wrong. Whether we had somehow introduced bacteria into the batch after brewing it (which was unlikely due to our Walter White-like attention to cleanliness during the process) or whether it was the mystery bag of only-meant-for-animal-consumption ingredients, something was seriously wrong. What had started out as an optimistic day to finally use our still turned into a disaster and a disposal mission. Drew's entire house smelled like we had slaughtered some chickens in it a week ago and simply forgot to clean up the mess. Luckily this was around lunch time, so we still had a few hours until his wife came home.

Considering that the batch at this stage is not all liquid but a soupy mixture of liquid and grain, we needed to throw it out somewhere as opposed to just down the drain. Besides, we didn't want any of that stuff touching anything else in his house. I had the brilliant idea to just take it to a communal dumpster for some apartment complexes nearby, halfway between Drew's place and mine. Well, the end result was that the whole neighborhood smelled for a few hours like it was hit by one of Saddam Hussein's SCUD missiles, except that it was filled with something even more vile than nerve gas. Both my roommates at home and Drew's wife hours later asked what the hell was going on in the neighborhood; they of course didn't find it as amusing as Drew and I did once they heard it was from us.

After that disaster we took our lessons learned and went over to the local home-brew beer and wine supply store to pick up some clean and fresh ingredients, made sure that all of our equipment and storage containers were super clean, and gave it another go. The result? Well, this time when we popped open the five-gallon container after the fermentation period, we were greeted with the delicious, sweet smell of grains fermented with champagne-style yeast. The alcohol percentage was somewhere in the 8-10% range: perfect! We finally had the chance to give our home-built frankenstill a go, and we were pretty excited. For those of you that are not familiar with the process, it is fairly simple. A still is basically a way to boil a liquid, collect the vapor that boils off, and then turn that vapor back into a liquid in a separate container. Alcohol has a lower boiling temperature than water, so the alcohol will boil off first and then be collected separately in another container, so it separated out and concentrated our 8-10% of alcohol from our initial brew into something much more potent.

After each distillation run your liquor will get more pure and higher in alcohol content. After the couple of runs that we did, we came out with something in the 160 proof (80% alcohol) range, which we then diluted with water to get down to what we wanted. One thing you'll also learn in the process is that if you get your still a little too hot, you'll start to get some boil-over seeping out of that not-quite-airtight shoddily-made still. Guess what happens when you have some high-test hooch boiling over onto a hot surface? Fire! Fortunately Drew's wife wasn't home for our initial run when we almost burned their house down, but everything worked out well in the end. We aged our booze with oak chips and it actually came out delicious! We did not start a distillery or brewery, but we had some fun, learned a lot in the process, and got drunk on some homemade booze.

Study Abroad & International Trips

      Who could forget about the beloved study abroad and international trips? Some of the best times that I had while doing my MBA were on these trips. They all will sound awesome and you will likely want to attend every trip that you can, especially if you are like me and have an itch for any type of travel, especially international travel. However, as soon as you start to think about the price tag of any of the potential trips, you will unfortunately be slapped in the face with the reminder that you are still a student and you will have some serious sticker shock. However, they are totally worth it, and I would suggest that you bite the bullet and attend at least one of them if you can.

      You will likely have multiple opportunities to go on trips, as our program always offered some type of trip during fall break, spring break, and the study-abroad summer trips. The trips will also vary by type of opportunity. A study-abroad trip is pretty self-explanatory; you'll study at another university and get credit for some classes. There will also be service trips where you are doing some type of community service work that is actually business-related (as opposed to building houses or something). There will be company-sponsored trips, where you are acting as a consultant for a company that either wants to expand to the location that you are travelling to or that is already operating there. Lastly, there will be more informational trips where you go on company and cultural site visits. The great thing about all of these trips is that most, if not all of them, should get you some type of class credit. Go on an awesome international trip and make one of your semester or quarter workloads easier? Sign me up!

Pre-Internship Summer Study Abroad in Germany:

I ended up doing two trips, both entirely different from each other. The first one was a three-week study-abroad trip to a tiny town in Germany that I cannot remember the name of. This was an interesting trip that involved a class at the local university of around thirty students (all from other MBA programs abroad), with a third to half of them being students from my home school. You will most likely see that you can do a study-abroad program at any school that offers one, but I would certainly suggest doing one at a school that your program already has a relationship with. The main reason is that it will be free or you'll get some type of reduced pricing. The program that we all attended in Germany was free for us but actually cost around $4,000-5,000 for the students that came from elsewhere, as their programs did not have a strong relationship with the local school. I could definitely feel the tension once this became known to the other students and found it hilarious when they were all stressing out about passing the final and making sure they got credit. I guess that's what happens when you drop $5,000 for a few weeks' worth of tuition. Don't be in their shoes, go somewhere cheap or free, as you will already be paying an arm and a leg for airfare, lodging, food, and any side trips that you end up taking.

From the academic standpoint, the classes were brutal. Not brutal in the hard or challenging sense, but just brutal in that classes were five days a week and you were expected to attend all of them. Oh, did I mention that they were for the entire day, as in full eight-hour days? Not my idea of fun. I was the douche that fell asleep for 60% of the lecture time, sometimes on purpose and sometimes because I literally could not keep my eyes open. I hate lectures. That being said, some of them were actually very interesting, covering topics around the European view of the financial crisis, case studies on great companies and their strategies, etc. We also generally had different professors every day, with a handful that covered a few days. There were no homework assignments for the most part, other than a group project, but there was a legitimate final that we all had to take and pass. It was open notes, though, and pretty much a joke, especially since for the summer classes my program didn't transfer over any GPA-affecting grades, so at least for the folks from my MBA program the class was pass/fail.

While the class days were horrible, this was still an awesome summer-abroad program. We did several really cool site visits that were related to the previous lectures. We got to tour an Amazon distribution center, an Audi manufacturing plant, some giant real estate projects, the European Central Bank's HQ in Frankfurt, and had some cultural visits to neighboring monasteries/wineries. I myself am a car guy, so I may have appreciated the Audi trip more than others, but it was pretty cool no matter what you're into. They had a museum there with some old cars as well as concept cars, but they also let us walk through the manufacturing plant where we literally got to see metal start from raw form in huge rolls of thin sheets all the way to the last stage of the process where they marry the engine to the chassis. The plant was full of self-driving fork lifts and automated welding robots -- tons of really cool technology to see! I was amazed at how automated the process was compared to some of the assembly lines you see at the American auto manufacturers.

I ended up doing this trip with one of my best friends from B-school, but was friends with or at least knew the others that came along from our program as well. My buddy and I started the trip off by going to London for the weekend, which ended up being just a day after Delta screwed us with mechanical errors and stranded us in Atlanta for the night. But let me tell you, we made use of that day! There aren't any memorable stories worth telling from the London trip, but I can say that the morning after was easily a top-three worst hangover. This may be attributable to the walk home from a club at 6am that ended up at a gas station to grab some milk and donuts. I of course had to best my friend somehow and ended up in a milk-drinking contest, basically against myself which I most certainly paid for the next day. The worst part of that was an agonizingly long subway -- or shall I say "tube" -- ride from the hotel to the airport, over the course of which I was trying to focus on breathing and trying to decide which of my nightmare scenarios was going to happen first, me projectile puking all over everyone on the crowded train, or violently shitting myself. Luckily for everyone else on the train I was somehow able to make it to the airport bathroom to take care of business.

The trip didn't get much better once we got to Germany. The town was just about an hour outside of Frankfurt and we were getting picked up at the airport by a driver hired by the school. A driver that knew the area (or so we thought), and who had the address of the awesome house that a few of us somehow scored to rent. Also, a driver that didn't know a lick of English. After we finally got to town just before dusk, the guy pulled up to a house, looked at the written address in his hand, looked back at the house, nodded approvingly, and dumped us off with our luggage. After the guy sped off, we tried to get in, but of course none of the keys worked. After a couple of searches around the house and for nonexistent street signs, we concluded this was most certainly not the place.

We walked into town a bit to the main street as it started to get dark and my buddy tried to pantomime our situation to some sweet old lady local restaurateur. Keep in mind that we were damn happy to see her and that she was still open, as it was a getting late on a Sunday night in a town that no doubt shows up as a speck of dust on any map of Germany, if at all. She took a few confused looks at the address and just pointed up a hill in the distance. We were in the heart of German wine country, where they make all of their Riesling, so imagine a landscape of rolling hills similar to Sonoma Valley, California. Anyways, there was apparently another small town a few miles up the hill, which is where she thought our house was. Fan-fucking-tastic! She called a cab for us, and as we were waiting for him, we saw our old cab driver rounding a corner. What the hell he was still doing there, as this was more than half an hour after he dropped us off, I have no idea. We shared a few awkward stares as we tried to wave him down, but I swear he hit the gas harder once he saw us. So much for that idiot actually finishing the job!

Summer time in rural Germany is absolutely beautiful, and even better considering that no matter where you go you can always find some fresh, locally brewed beer to enjoy at some outdoor patio or beer garden. I did not have a single day over the three weeks where I did not enjoy at least a couple of crisp, golden brown German Hefeweisens, with a few days where I probably enjoyed too many, like our last night where I was intrigued by a product I saw in a bar bathroom vending machine called a "pocket pussy". I think I made our server feel a little uncomfortable as I tried to slur out a conversation around how disappointed I was that the pocket pussy was sold out, considering that I had a long flight back the next day and all.

One of the great things about being on a trip like this over the course of several weeks is that it gives you time to take some fun side trips. Most of my weekend trips were within Germany, although we did take one trip to Switzerland. Probably one of the most fun trips we took was to nearby Frankfurt for the night before taking off for Switzerland. It was an interesting night overall, but was mostly fun because a few other guys that my buddy and I were friends with from school were also hanging out for the night before taking their own trip elsewhere.

Oddly enough there is a pretty good sized club at the bottom of the European Central Bank headquarters in Frankfurt that we had noticed when we did our site visit earlier. We ended up going there for the night since it was nearby and didn't take a whole lot of research on our part. Luckily for us the drinks didn't cost a left testicle the way they did at some of the other places we went to in Berlin or Switzerland. After some solid pre-gaming, we went to the club and continued to have shots poured as if they were free and sourced directly from the fountain of youth. The club was all right; it was actually pretty entertaining for me to watch my buddy continue to strike out talking to girls. He encountered two types: ones that didn't speak English, and ones that did, but that just weren't interested and would pretend to not speak English after a minute or so of conversation.

There were four of us out that night, and we all stayed at the same place, so we ended up walking back together. It wasn't long into the walk before we realized that we were in a pretty strange area. Pretty strange as in *really* strange. I am pretty sure I saw a few people shooting up some heroin in the doorway of a closed-down shop, and we saw some other guy, who seemed to be moving in slow motion, getting beat down publicly by some other guy out on the street. Turned out there was a red light district smack dab in the middle between the ECB building and our hotel. Well, a good portion of the group had girlfriends and overall we weren't exactly interested in sampling the goods for sale, but we did notice that there were also a few strip clubs. Now that was definitely something that we were interested in going to! Who doesn't want to wind the night down with a few casual beers while you watch women dance for you? Only issue was, the smallest euro paper bill is five euros (about $7 or so). Were we supposed to throw one-euro coins at the ones we liked?

Well, we ended up not having that problem. We certainly *had* a problem...it just wasn't *that* problem. After entering one of the "strip clubs" we all got a few beers and started to survey our surroundings in our drunken stupor, as if we just woke up dazed in a room filled with fog. The place was actually a dive, with just one small stage in the center. Kind of odd, but okay, no big deal. Anyways, we were all enjoying our beers and talking to a few of the girls that worked there about our trip so far, where we were from, just making conversation and enjoying our beers. So the server came over and one of the girls asked one of the guys in our group if we would buy them drinks. "Sure," he said, "no problem." I instantly realized that this was most certainly going to be a problem somehow, but decided to wait it out and see.

Our server came back with a few more beers for us and put some crazy-looking drinks that had about four or five different colors swirled around in the glass in front of each girl, along with some poker chips next to each drink. "What the hell is that?" said one of the other guys. Before I could give him an answer as to what my guess was (which was correct) the old lady behind the bar demanded, "Okay, now pay me for my drinks!" Pointing at the drink in front of each girl, she said, "Forty euro, forty euro, forty euro, forty euro! That with the beers comes to 180 euro!" Everyone was kind of stunned for a second, then one of the guys, Josh, whose turn it was to buy the round and who agreed to get the girls' drinks, said, "Whoa, what's in those drinks, cocaine?!" The girls started explaining that we weren't actually paying for the drinks, we were paying for their time, and that there are rooms behind the stage. Ah, so there's the catch. This is not a strip club after all, just a brothel in the red light district made to appear to be a strip club.

We ended up arguing with her for a second, saying that we'd pay a reasonable amount for the girls' drinks (which probably didn't even have any alcohol in them) and our beers but that there was no way in hell we were going to pay that. "Okay, so you're not going to pay?" the old lady said, then called out some guy's name real loud. All of the girls were now pleading with us to just pay and have a good time with them and not to cause any trouble. Nope, sorry sweetie, not going to happen. A minute or two later, from the door behind the stage where the back rooms were, appeared a giant, 'roided-up meathead that could have been Ivan Drago's shorter cousin. He tried to "persuade" us into paying the bill, but we stood our ground and offered up sixty euros, which seemed fair for eight beers and four drinks that may or may not have been water with some crazy food coloring in them. After a few more minutes of him trying to threaten us and block the door along with their doorman, I think he realized that his choices were to either take the deal we offered or throw down with their two against our four and destroy that tiny ass club in the process.

They ended up taking the deal and we all started to walk out. I was the last one in line and once everyone was outside but me, the guy threw his arm up in front of me blocking the way, demanding another five euros. "Sorry buddy, not getting it from me, we already gave you your sixty," I said. I won't go through the whole conversation, but it basically came down to a heated argument of him claiming we agreed on sixty-five euros and me basically saying, "Fine, if you want to fight me over a five- euro difference then I'm game,' 'cause you're not getting it." I may have sounded tough and gave him pause simply because I was taller and do hit the weight room when I can, but I think what helped me the most is that even after drinking myself stupid for the night I always outwardly seem somewhat sober. Truth is if we had ended up throwing hands I would have gotten my ass handed to me in about two seconds by that guy, but luckily for me he wasn't willing to find out over five euros. Even funnier was after we got outside my friends told me that they had actually negotiated sixty-five euros and not sixty like I thought -- oops!

Fall Break in Turkey:

The second international trip that I went on was a week-long trip over fall break that fell into the informational category. While there was no actual deliverable for the class or any type of exam, we did get credit. The trip was to Istanbul, Turkey and consisted of several site visits a day for the five days that we were there. Luckily, one of our professors is from Istanbul, so he played a big part in organizing the trip and knowing great tourist things to do, places to eat, etc. Leading up to the trip we had a few night lectures to go over the culture and the business environment there. Some of these were pretty interesting, but I think they were done more as a formality to give some legitimacy to the credit that we would be getting for the trip.

As expected for a trip with no real deliverables, the entire thing was a complete boondoggle. The only thing that was expected of you was to make sure you were on the bus in the morning, and for some people (myself included one day) even that was too much to ask! We were "chaperoned" by two of our professors, who came along for the daily site visits as well as the dinner and cultural events. Overall I would say there was a good mix of events, with some of the cultural and tourist events consisting of visiting the Grand Bazaar, a night boat cruise with dinner and a show along the Bosphorus, a visit to the Blue Mosque, and a visit to the Topkapi Palace, which was once home to the Sultans of the Ottoman Empire. The business trips consisted of visiting a Turkish University R&D biotech lab, the Turkish Stock Exchange (who knew one existed?), a tech company that is essentially the Yahoo of Turkey, as well as several others which I can't remember because they likely were on the day that I couldn't drag my ass out of bed to make the bus. I blame the hour and a half of sleep I got that night for that one.

One thing that we learned in our night lectures prior to the trip and quickly once we hit the ground in Turkey is that this is a culture that is huge on negotiating. Great for some of us on the trip, not so great for others that came along. Our first experience was on our first night in town, when a few of us met up for the night to go out to a bar/club per the recommendation of our Turkish professor. After walking around trying to find the damn place we finally got into a cab and told the guy where we were going. This dude did not have a meter, so he negotiated a fare with us. I think it came out to around $20 or so, not too terrible to split four ways, or so we thought. As we had no clue where the place was, we thought we were quite a bit away. Well, we got in the cab, the guy literally drove two blocks up in a straight line, stopped the car, and happily pronounced that we were there! We had missed the place because the entrance was set off a ways in an alley. Uh, what? Sorry sir, I don't care about what we settled on previously, but there's no way in hell you're getting $20, which can go a long ways in Turkey, for two blocks. Even though he was clearly screwing us he didn't seem all that happy with the $8 or so equivalent that we "renegotiated" for and gave him, which I think we all felt was still more than fair. Oh well, lesson learned!

So we finally made it to our spot for the night, which was called Club Roxy. The inside of the club was a bit odd; we couldn't quite tell if it was just the way clubs were in Turkey or if this place hadn't been updated since our old professor likely frequented it thirty years ago. Regardless, we were determined to get rowdy. It was our first night in town and the next day was to start late since some people were arriving in the morning. Drinks were cheap as hell, and a few hours into the night one of us realized that the tickets we were given with our cover charge were actually for free bottles from the bar. Guess what the free drinks were? Sex on the beach! So here we all are, feeling pretty good already, and now we each have a full 750mL-sized bottle of some glowing, fluorescent pink sex on the beach.

There were four of us to start, and eventually a fifth found her way to the club to meet us. We were all friends, but one of the guys was fairly new to going out with us, so the rest of us knew what type of shenanigans to expect from each other, but not this guy. Well, apparently he liked to slap people and roughhouse after a few drinks. Perfect, just what we needed. Our new friend Danny apparently slapped my buddy Mike a little too hard, as they almost broke out into fisticuffs in the bar. This caught the attention of the security guards at the club, who seemed to outnumber the patrons. What was almost a fight within our group of guys turned into another almost-fight between the whole group and the security guards, with me and one of the bouncers each holding each other by the collar. Luckily we were quickly able to diffuse the whole situation and assured them that we were good, no need to kick Danny out as he's not drunk and won't cause any more issues. Well, that was a good line until, as everyone started to back off and soften up their aggressive postures, all eyes were on Danny to see if he was all right. He literally took one step forward towards the bar and fell face first, ending up completely laid out on the floor! What an idiot; fortunately, they let us stay and continue to pound down our manly pink sex on the beaches.

Our next experience with negotiating in Turkey came at Danny's expense. We weren't all that concerned for him, since after the prior night we figured it was some quick-acting karma, plus it gave us priceless material to rag on him about for the rest of the trip. He wanted to buy some cologne and, what would you know, there happened to be a street vendor, a. k. a. homeless man, walking around with a bag of cologne boxes, selling cologne right outside the hotel. He negotiated for two bottles, and then we all headed into the lobby. I don't remember the exact prices now, but he felt pretty good about himself. He actually used to be a car salesman prior to coming to school and was very successful, being the top sales guy not just in his dealership or state, but in his region. Well, for being such a great fast-talking salesman, I have never seen someone fail so miserably when it comes to being on the other end of a deal.

As he walked back into the hotel, a woman and her husband were checking out. She noticed the bottles and asked, "Did you buy those from the man outside?"

"Sure did," said Danny.

"Do you mind if I ask how much you paid for the two of them?" asked the lady. Well, it turned out that she had just bought two similar bottles from the same guy earlier in the day, and paid about half of what Danny did! To add insult to injury, Danny took notice after the conversation and realized that the guy gave him the perfume version of what he was looking for, and not even the men's cologne. I don't know which one bothered Danny more, the deal he got or the fact that we were all busting out laughing once he realized he bought perfume. We affectionately referred to that situation as Danny getting "cologne guy-ed" for the rest of the trip.

Then there's Nick, who's one of those guys with no filter and a pretty disturbing sense of humor, much like mine actually. He grew up in the hood and loves to talk about his past experiences being in a gang and earning money in some less than legal ways. While he's the first to admit that he's no Brad Pitt, but he always seems to manage to find a few ladies that are into him. Apparently this was an issue for him one night on the trip, as he was trying to get back into the hotel late as hell with one of his new lady friends that he picked up. However, the hotel staff wasn't having it for some reason and wouldn't let him bring in his new acquaintance. I don't know if it was because they thought she was a prostitute or if they actually do have a no-guest policy after some time in the evening. In either case, he was clearly not happy about this.

Most of the group from the trip, and thankfully none of our professors, found out just how unhappy he was as we were leaving. Most of us had flights out at the same time, so the hotel had arranged a van to take us to the airport. There were probably eight or so of us in the van, half of us having known Nick for a while, with the others being first years in the program that generally didn't know him well at all considering fall break is only two months into the academic year and most first years don't have classes with second years until the second or third quarter. Anyways, we were all in the van and it wasn't leaving, and we were wondering what the hell the holdup was. Well, we found out once the front desk man from the hotel came out and, as nicely as possible, asked Nick to pay his dry cleaning bill before we left. Apparently Nick had had his suit and some other clothing dry cleaned by the hotel, and owed them $60 or $70. You wouldn't believe how quickly he flew off the handle at their request.

I won't go through the whole conversation here, but Nick started off by explaining that he didn't owe them any money and that he didn't know anything about the dry cleaning. After the guy politely asked him again to please pay the bill, Nick started to really get angry and say that they didn't even do a good job with the dry cleaning, that his suit and clothes were still all wrinkled and dirty. I was sitting right next to Nick in the back of the van and could smell how drunk he still was. I don't even think he actually got any sleep the night before; he was practically delirious and foaming at the mouth! After Nick admitted to having the dry cleaning done but that it was done poorly, another friend of ours started to plead with him to just pay the bill so we could all get to the airport. You could cut the tension in the air with a spoon at this point, with the first years just sitting up straight, staring blankly ahead and unmoving, as if they had a drill sergeant yelling and spitting in their faces. I was just trying to contain my composure and not start cracking up at the whole situation, because I knew that the hotel guy's politeness and insisting that he was just doing his job was only enraging Nick further.

Finally Nick's real beef with the hotel came to light as he started to go on a rant directed at this guy about how they wouldn't let him bring a girl back one night and he had to go pay for a hotel room somewhere else. You should have seen the performance that Nick put on. He threw the equivalent of $20 or so at the guy, mostly in change since, like most countries, Turkey uses coins for smaller denominations, as he said, "This is all I have and all you're going to fucking get."

"Sir, this isn't enough, we can't let you leave. Please just pay your bill. You got the dry cleaning done, I'm just trying to do my job," the hotel guy stammered out.

Wrong answer! Nick tried to crawl out of the back of the third row of the full van and lunge at the guy as he threatened physical harm and called the guy racist names (that don't even apply) that probably would have gotten his white ass shot back where he grew up. Our friend who initially pleaded with Nick to just pay the bill finally had enough and threw herself between the two of them, pulling out her purse to settle the difference of $40 or so. Problem solved. That was the quietest that I had ever seen those first year students, as we didn't hear a peep out of them for the rest of the ride, probably for fear of somehow enraging the lunatic in the back seat. Meanwhile, the rest of us were laughing about the situation for the whole ride back, some nervously, and some getting actual enjoyment out of the show!

Full-Time Recruiting & Negotiating Offers

I'll try to keep this section brief since 99% of what I mentioned for the different areas of internship recruiting will apply to full-time recruiting as well. If you are really interested in this stuff, as you should be since it will directly affect your bank account every month and may be a key skill for some of your future jobs, there will likely be a negotiation class offered as an elective that you should definitely take. There are entire classes and books devoted to the subject, so while this section will certainly not be exhaustive, it should cover the basics to get you on your way to getting more than what is initially offered.

Luckily, some of you will not even need to undergo full-time recruiting if you receive an offer from your internship that you want to accept. That being said, even if you are in that position, you should still go through the recruiting process. Why, you might ask? This comes down to one simple, beautiful (when you're the one who has it) word. Leverage. If you are given an offer during your summer internship or shortly thereafter from the place that you did your internship, the first thing that you should ask for is time. You may be given a reasonable amount of time to accept from the start, or they might tell you something ridiculous like two weeks. Whatever the case is, make sure that you have enough time to get through some of the full-time recruiting process with other companies, even if you know you will end up accepting the offer given because you liked the company, the city, or whatever your reasons are. They'll of course be pushing you hard to accept the offer and resisting giving you time, but this will be for the same reasons that you are asking for time. You want to put yourself in a better negotiating position, and they of course do not want to contribute to putting you in a position to squeeze some extra dollars out of them. One caveat here is that asking for time will make sense in a lot of situations, but not all. For example, if you don't get your first job offer until three months after graduation and don't have any interviews on the horizon, if it's something that you plan on accepting then just do it. You are outside of the normal recruiting window and should probably jump all over that thing as if it were a kid on Christmas morning who just got the green light to tear into the presents.

One thing that I shouldn't have to mention, but will, is to be very positive in your interactions and negotiations with your company. I suggest doing them over the phone, even though a lot of people who are shy or afraid of negotiating will be tempted to do this through email. Don't -- just suck it up and pick up the phone. They'll know why you want more time and question if you really want to work for them, so I like to frame up this conversation along the lines of saying how appreciative you are and excited about the offer from them, but that you want to make sure you have enough time to think about things and make sure that you are making the right decision, since you are thinking about a long-term career and this choice is a big one for you. You will typically be given more time to accept an offer that comes from an internship as opposed to the normal full-time recruiting process, simply because the offer from your intern company will come early in the year. It's not uncommon to be given several months to mull it over; you may not get the same amount of time through traditional recruiting, although a couple of months is not uncommon there either.

While you have time to accept your offer, you need to be laser-focused on going through the process with other companies to get other offers and see what you really want to do. Whether you are trying to get as many offers as possible to go after the best one, or if you are targeting just a couple of companies that are in the industry or city that you want to be in, you need to be focused. You will only have a few months of prime recruiting season and this may be one of the only times in your life where you are in the position of having huge, well-known companies vying for your attention and throwing dollars at you as if you were an all-star recruit about to go play pro ball.

The full-time recruiting season is where you may start to notice things becoming a little less amicable between classmates at school, as some people will be having a rough go of it and will be desperate for jobs. For the most part everyone will know who got what offers and who is likely to accept what offers. There will be resentment, but pay it no attention; this is your time to do what is best for *you*. Some people may start to hate you other than just jealously if you receive an offer that everyone knows you are likely to accept, or if you already have several offers, and they see you continuing to apply for postings and going out to interview for the same companies that they are. If you get an interview and they don't, or you move to the second round or get an offer and they don't, they'll be thinking that they missed out on a job they really liked because you are just trying to get some negotiating leverage and don't care about that job anyways. Well, that may be true, but it isn't your fault if they can't compete well enough to get an interview slot or an offer. This is most certainly a time for survival of the fittest.

When it comes to negotiating your offer, be creative and remember that everything is on the table. You can negotiate on base salary, annual target bonus percentage, stock options, signing bonus, relocation reimbursement, amount of paid time off days per year, anything your little heart desires. Do remember, though, that just because you ask for something does not mean that you will get it, and often times companies' hands are tied as far as what they can budge on and how far they can budge on it due to internal policies. For example, some consulting and law firms have set salaries and bonuses that they bring each year's new recruiting class in at, take it or leave it. Others have free reign to offer what they want; company structure, culture, and size will play into this.

As far as asking for specific things and talking numbers, I always like to try to see what they can offer first before coming up with a number on my own. With that being said, use data and facts to your advantage here, as this is really going to be a main tool for you. Someone will probably not give you an extra $5,000 a year because you tell them that you want it. However, they may give you an extra $5,000 a year because you tell them that you want it, *and* that you have another offer for that amount or that their offer is around $5,000 below the other offers for your class average. The most compelling data point you will have is that from another offer, and do not be ashamed to let them know that you have something else on the table. The next best data point will be those salary statistics that your school publishes and that you likely drooled over while writing your initial application essays. If they can't give on one point, try to work them on anther. For example, I know people that were not able to get their company to budge when it came to starting salary; however, they were able to get their company to double the signing bonus that was initially offered.

Out of all the data out there, there will likely be a counter-point to slice it in ways that are unfavorable for you. Just be reasonable in the way that you frame up your argument and use good judgment to ensure that you aren't overreaching. You may argue that in general the salary offered is lower than the class average, and they may argue that the data shows 60% of your class went into consulting and investment banking; fields whose notoriously high salaries likely skewed your data (assuming you are not negotiating with a consulting firm or investment bank). Use more specific data if possible, since that will be harder to refute. The best sources of data will be the already-mentioned school salary statistics from prior classes, published CPI indexes to help get a sense of cost of living in specific cities compared to each other, and even websites like Glass Door to some extent to ensure that you're in the ballpark for the company, industry, and specific role. The career coaches at your school can certainly help you with framing up your negotiating strategy, and they'll have a good pulse on what other companies or even what your offering company in the negotiation has offered recently or in the not too distant past.

Even people at the company you are negotiating with can be a resource. If there are some people there that you made a strong connection with or alumni from your program that you have spoken with in the past, they can be good sources of information. This is definitely something that you would need to sort of tiptoe around and feel them out on at first to see if they are comfortable discussing it with you or giving advice, but I have found that for the most part alumni genuinely enjoy helping out when given the chance and, unless they are the hiring manager or person that you are negotiating with, they'd likely rather see a few extra bucks end up in your pocket every year as opposed to on the bottom line of a company that they don't own.

Life After Graduation

First off I need to say congratulations for surviving the gauntlet and hopefully finishing school with an amazing offer! As far as the life after graduation part, wouldn't you like to know? Well, stay tuned for the **Fortune 500 Survival Guide!**

Printed in Poland
by Amazon Fulfillment
Poland Sp. z o.o., Wrocław